DI014340

RATITUDE

GRATITUDE

➤><+

Poems by
Sam Hamill

BOA Editions, Ltd. ➤> Rochester, NY <+ 1998

LC #: 97–74815
ISBN: 1–880238–65–9 paperback
ISBN: 1–880238–64–0 limited edition

First Edition
98 99 00 01   7 6 5 4 3 2 1

Publications by BOA Editions, Ltd.—
a not-for-profit corporation under section 501 (c) (3)
of the United States Internal Revenue Code—
are made possible with the assistance of grants from
the Literature Program of the New York State Council on the Arts,
the Literature Program of the National Endowment for the Arts,
the Lannan Foundation, the Sonia Raiziss Giop Charitable Foundation,
the Eric Mathieu King Fund of The Academy of American Poets,
as well as from the Mary S. Mulligan Charitable Trust,
the County of Monroe, NY,
and from many individual supporters.

Cover Design: Daphne Poulin-Stofer
Cover Art: Morris Graves, *Little Known Bird of the Inner Eye*, 1941,
tempera on paper 19" x 34½", Courtesy of Schmidt-Bingham Gallery.
Typesetting: Richard Foerster
Manufacturing: McNaughton & Gunn, Lithographers
BOA Logo: Mirko

BOA Editions, Ltd.
Richard Garth, Chair
A. Poulin, Jr., President & Founder (1976–1996)
260 East Avenue
Rochester, NY 14604

*for Gray Foster and Eron Hamill,
and for Bill and Kris*

Gratitude

*Whatever it is,
I cannot understand it,
although gratitude
stubbornly overcomes me
until I'm reduced to tears.*

—*Saigyō*

Contents

The Nets

Lives & Works

Preface: Ars Poetica

Some say the poem's
best made of natural speech
from the inner life.
I say, This is sometimes true.
The poem's a natural thing.

Some say the poem
should rise into purest song,
a formality,
articulate expression
achieved through complex structures

derived from classics—
which also is true enough.
Let the song arise
as it will. Learn to revise
the life. Beware. Disguises

rise up everywhere:
most dangerously, self-in-
fatuation. "More
poets fail," Pound declared,
"from lack of character than

from lack of talent."
Some insist the poem is
heaven-sent, claiming
angelic heirs. The poem,
I believe, is a failure

elevated in-
to triumph, a form of truth
wrought from mortal flesh
and blood that will soon perish,
but which—for one brief moment

or an hour—reveals
the tragic human spirit
in the very act
of imagining itself
cured of the sickness of self.

The poem cannot,
finally, be explained nor
defined. The true gift
poetry bestows begins
and ends with humility

before the task. All
the suffering of this world
can be truly felt,
absorbed and transcended, just
by the act of listening

to that deepest voice
speaking from within. Forget
hagiography.
All the great masters are dead.
Forget rime and irony.

Forget words, meter,
diction, whole syllabaries—
the literary.
The heart by way of the ear.
What's that you wanted to say?

→>-<←

Three Worlds

The Fool:
A Letter to Paul Hansen

When Bodhidharma
came from the West, for nine years
he sat, face-to-wall.
A student asked old Yang-chi,
"What could this possibly mean?"

"He was Indian,"
Yang-chi replied with a grin,
"he spoke no Chinese."
Chuang Tzu says, "If you follow
dictates of an accomplished

heart, then you have found
a teacher. And who can fail
to find a master?"
When I set out for Yueh,
I never dreamed I would find

myself in shadows
of ancient masters whose trails
wind ever deeper
into dark mountain shadows
before the burgeoning dawn.

"He who knows enough
to stop at what he does not
truly know is there."
Well, old friend, let me be first
to confess to wandering

still. The world is filled
with scholars who do not know
that the poetry
is only glimpsed through the words
like a lover undressing

behind the shōji
screen, her lovely silhouette
mistaken for her
body. Poetry is not
the fact of her living flesh

nor the old longing
stirred in the loins by a glimpse
of neck-nape or breast.
The poem is shaped by words
the accomplished heart holds dear,

and, composed by ear,
says much more than words can say.
Take away the words,
and there is still poetry.
Facts merely get in the way.

I have surrendered
to the mystery of it all.
My face to the wall,
mountains and rivers remain.
I am a fool, Paul, to have

thought for a moment
I could stop the moon mid-sky,
that I could embrace,
if only for a moment,
the moon reflected in your eye.

And yet I persist
as the trail winds more deeply—
as I'm aptly named:
Obaka-san the Pilgrim,
a happy fool following

the light reflected
by the eyes of ancient fools,
crumbling old Buddhas,
Taoist loonies—to the point:
people who are just like you.

-+->-<+-

After Po Chu-i

Winds toss up white wavecaps
like ten thousand flowers.

Dark geese against a clear, blue sky
as if written in Chinese.

-+->-<+-

Three Worlds

From the split, dry trunk
of a three-hundred-year-old
tsubaki tree, one
fragile new twig with three leaves
holds a perfect red flower.

→>-<←

The Art of Literary Exegesis

They argued, the three of them,
for three long hours—were arguing
when I, eventually, went home—
over the "meaning" of the poem.

It was almost morning.
There were dozens of morning birds,
gray doves, and when they sang,
their meaning and their love

were not in words.

—>—<—

The Art of Literary Translation

1.
Asking one who is
not a poet to translate
poetry is like
asking a heart surgeon to
repair your brakes—every

once in a while, you'll
find one who can do it well.

2.
Squabbling as they will
in busy traffic, two crows
make meals of road kill.

-+->-<-+-

Anti-Muse

There are people who take on a kind of
weird glow—like a fish left out
for a week; there are people who suck
all the air from a room just by breathing.

At midnight, even the stars begin to cower,
measuring this silence for hours.
There are people who write verse
who beat all the life out of words.

→-◄-

After Yuan Chen

The beautiful face
of the Seductress of Wu,
where could it have gone?
Into the grains of wild grass
softly waving in spring winds.

→>-<-

Salutation, Late Autumn, 1991

It is late afternoon, the beginning
of the darkest month of the year, evening
trembling in the shadows. I stoke the fire,
heat a small pot of sake, and open
for the first time Bashō's
Narrow Road to the Interior fresh
from the printer.
                The world remains unchanged:
the moon emerges from a bank of clouds,
shining wetly through the trees. Now I read
the words I fashioned from the Japanese
of a friend three hundred years my senior.
And drink, embracing his same solitude.

Today, the world's good. I raise a cup:
what I love most, I have given away.

⇥⇤

A Warbler's Song in the Dusk

after Yakamochi

I crossed an ocean
dappled by high drifting clouds
blown on winter winds
to hear the warbler's solo
stir old memories of my vows.

★

Little Japanese
uguisu, little warbler
singing in the dusk,
do you remember lovers,
is that why you sing for us?

★

The plum blossoms fall,
soon the cherry trees will bud.
Someone plays piano
in a house not far away.
And your sad soprano calls.

★

A car on the road,
the noise of growing cities—
even one small bird
returns the human spirit
to ancient joys and pities.

★

Millions of people
in cars and trains and subways
buy and sell and trade—
one lonely warbler singing,
and we give our hearts away.

*

Uguisu, your song
and your name are one.
A moment alone—
listen to your song, it's true—
and the soul sings out again.

→-◄-

Two Pines

1. Yung Chia Reconsidered

A wind in the pine,
moonlight trembling on the stream
at deepest midnight
on the coldest evening:
what does it mean.

2. Hakutsu's Pine

A great pine stands close
beside the old stone house.
Examined in detail?
Like meeting ancient sages
face-to-face.

→>-<+

After Han Yu

Almost fifty-four,
and suddenly pills appear:
this for allergies,
and this for my bad stomach;
calcium for crumbling teeth,

a melatonin
when I can't sleep; vitamins
when I can't quite eat.
My hearing aid is a gift—
now I can listen to music,

and still remove it
when the talk grows tiresome or
I'm lost in the din.
I can't see a thing close-up
without my glasses. My back's

shot from bucking wood.
My arthritic hands are stiff.
I've a smoker's cough.
I've petrified my liver
with sake and tequila.

I need arch supports
in my shoes, and my bum knee
sometimes needs a cane.
My body's a litany
of small, nagging aches and pains.

That's the way it is—
not much good for anything,
and I'm not even
old! Thirty years ago, drunk
on the wine of the classics,

I wanted to age,
I wanted a sparse white beard
and a haggard face.
I've earned it. It's mine. So what?
Still need wood for the fireplace.

→>-<+-

Ten Thousand Mirrors of Happiness

How I love the wine
made from the rice of Japan's
snow country. When chilled
on a warm spring night, it soothes
both mind and palate and prompts

good conversation.
Drunk hot in an evening chill,
it warms heart and bones
and stimulates the flavor
of soup, spicy hot chicken,

good *ohitashi*—
steamed spinach with tuna flakes.
And there's poetry
when it begins to get late,
or some funky downhome blues
or late-night *shakuhachi*.

Po Chu-i, Li Po,
and Tu Fu often got by
drinking milky dregs.
Ikkyū sang of its virtues,
Bashō indulged its pleasures.

I follow footsteps
made by ancient masters.
I keep my pleasures
simple: good food and rice wine,
and the world is plentiful.

Friends think me crazy,
but I prefer good sake

to the finest wines
of Europe. So: *Ten Thousand
Mirrors of Happiness! Kompai!*

-+>-<+-

By the Rapids

after Sugawara Michizane

I abhor noisy places,
yet adore this tumbling creek.

The hermit turns on his pillow,
the old string is strummed.

An old pine, an umbrella on the bank,
blowing leaves, moored boat rocked by waves:

nothing needs my attention tonight
but "Free and Easy Wandering" in my *Chuang Tzu*.

→►◄←

Lives of a Poet:
Two Songs for Takamura Kotarō

1.
Down the hills from Hanamaki,
across rice fields deep in snow all winter
or glistening in the summer moon,
the little house of Kotarō stands beside a pool,
behind a few trees and a flower garden.

The war is over. Chieko's dead.
Is the old man shamed—is that why
he bows his head to carve from tough wood
this small bird, beak shut tight, the
loneliness of mountains in its eyes?

The smell of Chieko's plum wine
lingers like smoke through the night.
The summer cicadas have gone. Only trees
and stars. Kotarō, motionless, listens.
This silence is almost enough.

2.
The old Jōdō temple, Shoanji,
a bombed-out relic in Hanamaki,
was never much more
than a two-tatami shed,
paper doors

and wooden Buddha
carved by a farmer or priest.

Now, another forty years gone,
it's a dark skeleton

beside the narrow highway, old bones
refusing to be buried.

Car after car rushes by,
drivers bored and in a hurry.

→>-<-

Along the Way

Dusty, sooty city. Busyness
everywhere. Young women in perfume
and paint and fancy underwear.
Noisy, piped-in rock 'n' roll.

Blue dusk of a winter afternoon,
hands warm deep in empty pockets,
I look in all the windows
at nothing I want, nothing I require.

No ambition, no complaint.
"Strive and strive," the Master asked,
"what is it that you seek?"
No fear. No need. Happy without desire.

→>-<-

Talking to Myself

for Robert Aitken

Gazing at the moon,
you lose the pearl in your hand,
the old saying goes.
In the *Discourses of Chao*
it is written, "The body

of reality
is common to all Buddhas;
all people have it,
but do not realize it
because it's deeply buried

under illusions."
The cycle of samsara
endures in the hearts
of those who seek nirvana.
Give up all enlightenment!

You are almost there.
Everywhere a Buddha sits
is the Lion Throne.
Try, just try to get it wrong!
It's like trying to chew air.

No matter how far
you may wander, there you are.
Chao-chou departed
wearing sandals on his head.
Disputation goes nowhere.

The road to T'ai Shan
enters the bowels of hell
where demons of self

devour the soul. Old Chao-chou
still had to see for himself.

The Madman of Ch'u
declares, "The sage does sage deeds.
Good fortune is light,
yet none can put on its wings;
misfortune's heavy as earth,

none can escape it.
Oh, be done!" he cries, "be done
with drawing people
on by your virtue's power!"
He says, "My tracks run crooked

but don't hurt my feet."
The way is mysterious,
and you're still groping
for light in the dark, the pearl
bright as the moon in your hand.

→>-<-

Lives & Works

Lives of a Poet:
A Letter to Adrienne Rich

How much you have changed
my life! It is breathtaking
to look back again
on the deep sickness of men
of my grim generation.

You scared us witless
often enough with your bold
commitment to truth
and uncommon decency.
I still know the man I was,

one who raised his hand
or voice against the very
thing he loved the most—
the sickness of self gnawing
away inside like a dog.

The answers I found,
I found as often as not
within your poems
and essays, or in Atwood's,
or in Simone de Beauvoir.

Poetry readings
against the Vietnam War
were everywhere, but
I was already a vet
and had become a c.o.

and still that sickness
waged war within me—to be
what, if not a man?
You brought me to see that grief,
like hope, belongs to us all.

What diminishes
a woman makes a man small
in equal degree.
More than thirty years have passed
since I first offered shelter

for battered women.
My wife opened a shelter
twenty years ago.
And yet the murders continue,
day after horrible day.

And despite it all,
we find peace at the center.
You have changed my world
and my perception of it
finally and forever.

Orphaned in this world,
I was born to this struggle:
a lifetime searching
for kinship, for becoming,
for endless transformation.

This revolution
has no beginning, no end.
What I most value
is most easily attained:
sustenance and gratitude.

"Gratitude" is such
a simple word, a verbal bow
I make with palms clasped,
Gasshō! "Yours with the Buddha."
"I dreamed you were a poem,"

you wrote a lover,
and I often think you, too,
are a long poem
whose gift is the gift of change,
of sublime transformation—

"If you're not part of
the solution," we all said,
"you are the problem."
And that's still as true today.
Your poetry *is* a Way.

"The poet today,"
you wrote in 'seventy-four,
"must be twice-born. She
must have begun as a poet,
she must have understood

the suffering of
the world as political, . . .
and on the other
side of politics she must
be reborn again as a

poet." To be born
again and yet again is
the poet's foremost
obligation. Audre Lorde
said it: "Poetry is not

a luxury." It
is lifesaving, sustaining
what can't otherwise
be salvaged from the wreckage
of the American life.

→>−‹−

Passing Through

Kyō mo kyō mo
kasunde kurasu
koie kana

—Issa

Somewhere between Eugene and Portland,
wipers slapping time to an ancient folksong
I got on Sado Island in the Sea of Japan,
I thought again of my old friend
with whom I walked in the Rose Garden
on a sunny August afternoon
twenty years ago, walked and talked
the life of poetry as if it could be
almost a religious vow.

Rain pouring down
and hundreds of miles to go,
I pulled off the highway
and drove through town until I found
my way again and stopped in the garden
to sip hot coffee and smoke a cigarette.

He who was my brother is a stranger now.
Calls are unanswered. Letters are returned.
How does a man get up one day and simply
walk out of one life and into another
without a trace or track? How does the old bear
curl up inside itself to wade the wide
fields of heaven when rain turns to snow
and bitter glacial winds begin to blow?

It was hot that August afternoon.
Late into the night, there was poetry and wine.
We spoke of others we had loved and lost,
and I thought of how I passed
like shadow through their lives—

former friends, former wives—I wish them well,
although I do not know them now.
I make my bows alone.
It's easier loving the dead who blossom
in the mind like roses in the wind.

After months of rain, the roses will bloom again,
the old bear come creaking down its mountain.
And the old ache that is my memory now
picks up the tempo the wiper is laying down
as I pull back onto the highway out of town,
the women of Sado turning, stepping lightly
in another world, raising their arms
and voices once again to sing
that sweet old song that carries
a weary pilgrim home.

+>-<+

After Coltrane's "I'll Get By"

These autumn nights I think hard and long
on Wang Wei, ancient Chinese poet alone,
resigned behind his brushwood gate,
nothing at his door but the wind,
the same white clouds and mountains.

My old dog groans in his sleep.
The cold October moon fills my room with light.
I light a cigarette and pour a shot of tequila,
promising myself I'll clean up my act
next week.

Neither drunk nor sober,
something of Coltrane lingers
long after the music's over,
something of the loneliness that transcends loneliness,
like the emptiness of Wang Wei.

It tends to get very late.
Opening a book, I read a poem
in a voice that rasps in the night.
"A wretch needs his wretchedness," Roethke cried.
All right, all right. I'll to go to bed.

I got to be up
to greet the light.

-+->-<+-

Ish Province Worksong

The plan
is the work.

The work
is play,
joy,

wherein reside
silence
and song

side by side
lighting
the way.

→-→-←-

The Oracle at Sunrise

laborare est orare

The tall shadows of nightfall
slide back toward stately tall cedars
as first sunlight wavers through
a thick cream of fog. Crows call in the mist.

As uncertain as the first promise of morning,
I fit key to lock and the door swings wide,
and I breathe in the scents of ink, type wash,
and dry alder stacked beside the iron stove.

Dark banks of type anoint me with longing,
a silent reminder of saintly old masters: the Didots,
Bodoni, Claude Garamont, . . . Fournier, Morris
and Morison, Hermann Zapf and funky Fred Goudy.

Cloistered so in a temple of ambition, it is
the hour of black coffee and meditation, the hour
of breaking hearts through the mail and the kindling
of salvation: some days almost too much to bear.

The old platen press—no one uses them much
anymore—hums and chugs and clunks;
damp imported paper whispers through my fingers—
kisses from the dead.

The fire chuckles in the stove. The old dog
drowses near the door. And although I know
heaven is the dream of charlatans and fools,
I steady myself and begin my morning prayer.

➤—◄

Moon-Watching Pavilion

Two weeks ago, when daffodils bloomed
in huge, yellow blossoms, I stood with you
out on the Moon-Watching Pavilion
at the far end of our Japanese garden,

full moon pillowed in clouds, flowers
so pale in moonlight they seemed almost
memory, more dream than substance.
I knew it wasn't right, but I wanted to nail

the moon right there in the sky, a huge
zero high above our house drowning
in a pool of smoky cloud.
Now it is May, and truly spring,

weeping cherry lavender with buds,
pink flowers on wild currants, tulips
purple—almost black before they open.
Two rusty robins farm the edge of the garden.

*

In early May, midday, I take my zafu
out to sit on the pavilion. The *Kōshōji*
says outward attachment to form
results in inward confusion, "contact

with circumstances itself creates confusion."
All I can hear in the quiet afternoon
are a few gulls far out over the water
searching for the end of the sky,

a crow somewhere nearby, constantly chuckling.
I hear myself breathe a few breaths, and then
that, too, passes like a shadow. The gray cotton sky disappears.
"The flesh is the body, home to three Buddhas."

What use is *Kabbalah* or the Sutras?
In a week, a new moon emerges.
Yugen, the mystery. The body is a temple,
not a refuge. *Maha prajna paramita!*

+>-<+

Midsummer

Two yearling deer
stood in heavy falling mist
in the middle of

the road leading in-
to town, brown coats glistening,
huge eyes open wide,

caught in the headlights,
in the first yellowish smear
of coming daybreak.

Twenty feet away,
I finally stopped the car
and sat still inside,

eyes locked together
in a curious searching
with those of the doe.

Minute by minute,
we were transfixed, motionless,
each imagining

the other. And then
the sun peeled back the dark clouds
like a second skin,

and, in unison,
the deer stepped slowly forward,
gently, cautiously,

off the road, into
underbrush that flourishes
along the woods' edge

and vanished in mist.
Dazed, I returned to my day,
to the work at hand.

And now, the hour late
in the morning, mist falling
again, I can still

feel my skin prickle
under those beautiful brown
doe-eyes searching me

like a lover's hand,
cautious, slowly exploring
something deep in me

I cannot touch or name.

-+->-<+-

Lives of a Poet:
To Kenneth Rexroth

Solstice. Once again
the foreshortened days
and cold, clear nights of winter.
Last night, in freezing moonlight,
I paused at the woodpile
where it lay under frost,
I paused to look up
at the Dipper. It hung
so close I could almost
taste its froth, and suddenly,
for no reason I can name,
suddenly, I remembered
what you said to Williams
all those years ago
about a poet being one
who creates sacramental
relationships that last
always.

Bare alders glistened
in the dark, and the whole world
creaked beneath my step.
My own breath wafted
before me, and I thought
how certainly the diurnal
becomes the annual, how
wood shatters into flame
as I stoke December's fire.

Far to the south, the moon
pruned the tips of Olympic
spruce and cedar, then slipped
into snowy hills. In this land
you roamed so many years ago,
on this coast where you loved

your grief away
huddled near a fire on
the cold beach at Kalaloch
under the floating shadows
of wooden sculptures carved
by the broad hands of the sea,
we are at peace in the world
where the dirty hands of industry
find us too poor to exploit.

Again and again in this
season's bitterest cold,
I savor the sacrament
of your poems—always
those warm shadows of campfires
lingering on, odor
of sheepherder coffee, moonlight
sifting the trees. The music
of silence drifts up from
the vast, soundless sea.
And in the flux and flow of
soundless change unchanging,
Adi-Buddha dances, and I
am happily lost

in the dance of the Gopis
where poetry stands revealed.

→><←

Lives of a Poet:
A Letter to Gary Snyder

Nearly forty years
have passed since Kenneth Rexroth
introduced me to
the mountains and rivers of
your poems, the campfire light

flickering softly
across a page of Milton,
animal shadows
and wide, wise innocent eyes
observing from the darkness.

I was just a kid
with a heroin habit
and a talent for
self-destruction. Your poems
returned me to sanity—

as much as could be
at the time. Now poor Kenneth
has been fifteen years
in his grave, whose epitaph
I set and printed in his

The Silver Swan some
twenty years ago, not long
before your *Gaia*.
"Above Pate Valley," yellowed
with age and writ in a hand

imitating yours,
still remains in my office,
along with snapshots
of Kenneth in the Cascades
circa nineteen twenty-eight.

I no longer go
deep into the mountains, but
remember printing
your "Axe Handles" every time
I buck wood. Which is to say

nine bows to a friend
and teacher who encouraged
a lifetime's study.
The mountains are in my heart,
and all the rivers that flow

flow from headwaters
"going back roughly forty
thousand years, dating
from the early cave paintings,"
you remarked in Alaska

twenty years ago;
and, "About five thousand years
is all one human
mind can comfortably hold."
You've managed to redefine

civilization.
You have given us Stone Age
economics and
the idea of *practice*—
Buddhist and/or poetic—

you have given me
a model for my practice,
not something merely
to imitate, but a wise
counsel culled from the ages.

Now I'm no longer
young, though plentifully foolish—
my Japanese friends
have dubbed me *Obaka-san*—
and you're almost old enough

to be the tribal
elder you have always been.
"Mountains and rivers
without end." From an old scroll,
a single kernel of thought

blossoms forty years
from its inception, like that
hundred-and-twenty-
year cycle of some bamboo.
The poem becomes the life

in some respects, it
deepens our engagement with
all that is human,
with all this temporal world,
plagued by all-too-human greed.

Who will join Shiva
and Tara, Kokope'li
and Dōgen Zenji in
"the dance of the intellect
among the ten thousand things?"

What I want to say,
what I have struggled to say
in this poem, is
that you have been a master
and model, a friend and sage

for those who follow.
And if I may paraphrase:
That's what a poet
is—one who recognizes
sacramental relationships.

That is the real work—
reading books or bucking wood
or washing babies—
attentive lives all our days:
the real joy is gratitude.

→><←

Lives of a Poet:
Two Letters to Denise Levertov

1.
"I wanted to learn you by heart,"

I wanted the music of
        "your intense unmusical voice"
to carry the weight of the poem
        that carries us
toward the warm
        wet light of the hopeful:

poems
to remind us forever
        of Allende,
the way
        and reason
he died;
        or the pathetic beauty
and sadness of
        "those groans men make"
when a lovely woman passes—

as though they could sniff out
        the grace
of her compassion.

                    ★

And so I sit
        beside the woodstove, reading:
how easily I am pleased
        and how rarely!—the outer
warmth of the fire, the inner
        heat of the line.

Hungry
        for food as for justice,
I take the round vowels
        deep into my mouth,
my tongue
        and lips careful to arouse
each consonant between:

        that taste
        of the luminous dust.

                            *

And you give me and give me that
which I didn't know I had—

the bread of the knowledge
        of "suffering humanity"
we share as we carry,
        eating as we go. If

I may retrieve
        from these graces
some aspiration
        to inner joy and goodness,

shall I praise you
more highly than the Goddess?

                            *

My strong and willing elder sister,
        it's you and I must stand
against the murderous technicians:

        traffickers in arms
        and lives
        and wisdom; marketeers;
        all forms of theorists; careerists;
        and loathsome politicians.

In such moments of in-
          tense confrontation,
an absolute sureness
          comes over me
when the poem
          rides

          the *anemos*
          (breath or wind
          of in-
          spiration)

on which we glide and sing.

2.
Thinking, reading late
          your "Modulations for Solo Voice"
at the dead end of night,
          remembering Robert Duncan's great poem,
"My Mother Would Be a Falconress,"
          hunting back over
that same fertile ground—
          "groundwork" as in
Duncan's own grand testimonial—

seeking the various threads
          of a fabric the way a painter might study
the fragile elegance of
          Asian handmade paper,
eye alert to subtle
          inconstancies, studying the material
to become the material:
          the lonely soul the only empty canvas
the human heart must fill.

It is like loving an Anton Chekhov,
          an Akhmatova, a Su Tung-p'o—
the love is there and real,

a tangible in this brief
intangible world. Thus the voice,
        enthralled, has
no choice but to speak.
        Lu Chi dips
his brush because he must.

May a poet write *amor?*
        Was there ever
a mother who did not hum?
        Art is not
for. Art is mother of the soul,
        but no romantic vision
can dissuade the heart's own
        existential leanings.
The heart rises like a bird of prey
        and then returns,
humbled, to its hood.

Rice paper. Mulberry paper.
        A voice like gouache.
Moonset. It is all
        one thing.
I have stayed up so late,
        I may as well stay up.
The voice, like the heart,
        modulates.
It grows light.

⤙⤚

Little Epic Elegy

for Denise Levertov, 1923–1997

She is gone who brought
us closer to what we are,
who brought us a world—
a passion for the garden,
a heaven of moons and stars.

And now she attends
our days with the salts of truth
and all the honeys
of conviction. Her vision
returns us into a world

of mystery, awe,
all compassion and delight,
to joy in the work
of being fully human,
always picking up the torch,

passing on the light.

→►◄←

The Nets

The Nets

Somewhere someone is untangling
the heavy nets of desire
beside a small fire at the edge of the sea.

He works slowly, fingers bleeding,
half thinking, half listening, knowing
only that the sea makes him thirsty.

>-<-

Hitomaro's Song

Just how many nights,
despite my endless pleading,
have you refused me?
But to surrender my hope
is more painful than waiting.

->-<-

Many Happy Returns

"There is nothing," you said, "to return to
that has not been made holy." Inside
the soiled alba of the human breath,
the ancient order still resides—

I have returned to wander the distant
boundaries of your fingers where the eclogues
sing themselves a country for the heart.
It's not as easy as that.

If I had wanted only a measure, I might
have paused to tick the syllables away or
twisted this groan that passes for a voice
into what song, what agony of intention.

Boundaries, then, where nothing comes
between us. If I could open my body
like a gate, the pastures would rise gently
toward dark woods and tall shadows,

still, or slowly bending. What goes there
goes delicate—more delicate than speech
or brazen poetry. The heart is *not*
a gate. What opens stands ajar already,

a mat of welcome, a temple bell
whose tolling lingers long, long after
the clapper rests against still air.
When we return into our bodies,

our bodies change and change, candles
flicker in our eyes. This is the true
forgotten mass, the one order
of the ancient faith: this is the body

and holy; this is the body, eucharist of flesh,
its blessing the holy of holies for which
we return and return in the act of worship,
the act of faith unto death.

+>-<+

Dolphin Song

Your hands on my body
bring dreams of summer gardens,

islands with white beaches
where dolphins swim.

I drift under your fingers
like a shadow under water.

Whenever you touch me,
my whole body glistens.

+><+

Shunga

To Eleanor Wilner

In the blizzard's heart,
four days housebound in the snow,
translating Bashō
while in the towns and cities
boathouses collapse, roads close,

rivers overflow.
I take out Hiroshige's
shunga, a block print
of a slim woman grasping
her lover's huge erection.

"Does that turn you on?"
my wife wants to know. No.
And yes. I sometimes
dream of Hiroshige's hands
as they sought the wood's deep grain,

the knifeblade moving
like that of Ting the Cook from
Chuang Tzu, effortless
in evoking snow that falls
day after darkening day,

how his hands reveal
her so-startled expression—
so serious and
yet so comical as she . . .
I think of Hiroshige

carving through a storm,
mind focused on a woman
in the very throes
of—could it be ecstasy?
Or shocked or shameless, exposed

for herself to see
in the mirror of desire,
a grotesquerie.
And that man, her poor lover,
dwarfed by his own erection,

which does defy truth,
not logic, a great dragon
rising from its sleep
to search for satiation,
reptilian heat in winter.

What was he thinking,
Master Hiroshige, as
he shaped their eyes, lips,
and enormous genitals?
What complexity he caught,

innocence and lust,
what horror and devotion!
Outside, more snow falls.
I put the image away,
kiss my wife and stoke the fire.

In the blizzard's heart,
we fall like windblown snowflakes
until it is all
one thing, sexuality
and gender, the *yin* and *yang*

of one mind curling
up inside itself to snooze—
ah, perchance to dream!
of old unbridled passions
on a freezing New Year's Eve.

->-<-

Fire and Water

After you bathed
and powdered
and went away:

your cool wet towel
against my burning face

→>-<-

Lives of a Poet:
Ikkyū's Song of the Dream Garden

I. from the Chinese

1. *Song of the Dream Garden*

Pillowed on your thighs in a dream garden,
little flower with its perfumed stamen,

singing, sipping from the stream of you—
Sunset. Moonlight. Our song continues.

2. *Face-to-Face with My Lover on Daitō's Anniversary*

Monks recite the sutras in honor of the Founder,
their many voices cacophonous in my ear.

Afterward, making love, our intimate whispers
mock the empty formal discipline of others.

3. *My Hand Is Lady Mori's Hand*

My hand is Lady Mori's hand
and knows her mastery of love.

When I am weak, she resurrects my jeweled stem.
The monks I train are grateful then.

4. *Night Talk in a Dream Chamber*

Whether by sea or river or in mountains,
a monk in the world abandons fame and fortune.

Every night, we nestle like ducks in bed, sharing
intimate whispers, our bodies become at one.

5. *My Love's Dark Place Is Fragrant Like Narcissus*

At midnight, your face in a dream brings a sigh.
Ch'u's love pavilion was long ago and far away.

But like a blossom on the flowering plum,
sweet narcissus blooms between your thighs.

6. *Elegy*

We first lay down among flowers
ten years ago and found a timeless rapture.

Sadly, I remember being pillowed by her lap,
all-night love, all eternity in our vows.

II. from the Japanese

1.
Without beginning,
utterly without end,
the mind is born
to struggles and distresses,
and dies—and that is emptiness.

2.
Like vanishing dew,
a passing apparition
or the sudden flash
of lightning—already gone—
thus should one regard one's self.

3.
The moon is a house
in which the mind is master.
Look very closely:
only impermanence lasts.
This floating world, too, will pass.

4.
And what is mind
and how is it recognized?
It is clearly drawn
in *sumi* ink, the sound
of breezes drifting through pine.

→─◄─

Midaregami

Reading Yosano Akiko's *Tangled Hair*,
I find you everywhere:

In moonlight and rain, in lotus dew,
in Akiko's tangled hair.

All those ancient tragedies
and comedies in every little tune—

Sapphic. Catullan.
In every poem, you.

-÷-÷-

A Thousand and One Tales

I am lying naked, dreaming in bright sunlight,
on a blanket, on a small patch of lawn
hidden by a dense wall of cedar and spruce,
lying in a garden of blooming iris
where robins sing and crows complain,
sun warm as my wife's familiar hand
on my pale white butt, propped
on elbows, revising for the twenty-first time
an erotic story I began for her
last winter, but which somehow became
a tale of someone else, someone I invented
accidentally, out of my own pleasure
in inventing and out of the love
most men have of imagining, of
telling tales, of describing,
always describing the physicality
of their world of pleasure and the dance
of Eros free of guilt or consequence,
so that, as I lie here aroused yet again,
indulging the cheap thrill of ordinary lust,
enthralled again by this imaginary woman
who, despite looking and sometimes
talking very like my wife, is a creature
of my own imagining, and yet, lying here
alone, I must follow wherever she leads
as her tale unfolds and her lover, now
my alter ego, adoringly undresses her before,
say, an admiring, lustful semipublic,
undressing his own Psyche in the process
until I find myself imagining a character
in a drama imagining himself to be a writer
of gentle erotica imagining himself
in a play in which he portrays
the writer imagining his lover
imagining the dance of naked
Shiva and Shakti, of Krishna's

night of ecstasy with ten
thousand milkmaids, while the words
keep coming, keep coming—*breast, thigh,
erection*—in their own rising
and falling cadences, exact rhythms
of the breath that speaks so breathlessly
to the ear that listens closely so the
attentive eye may enter the dream
that returns us, finally, to the garden.

→>—<←

Epithalamion for Bill and Kris

Poised at the threshold of a dream,
it is good to look back once again.
For who could have dreamed, my brother,
when we were young so long ago,
this day would ever come? Could we
have seen through all our youthful zeal
that this day would finally come
when we too might achieve the calm
gray perspective of, say, Tu Fu,
poised late in life to consider
his long white beard, his demeanor
shaped by a lifetime's convictions.

Poised at the threshold of a dream,
my sister, it is also good
to assay the day's intentions.
"Something old, something borrowed, some-
thing blue." The dream, the vow, the ring
that represents completion and
sets the boundary the husband-
man patrols. Wife means wave, means veiled,
only to her soulmate revealed.
At the center of the flower,
a beauty born of emptiness—
the perfection of wisdom—ah!

Poised at the threshold of a dream,
the poets and philosophers,
the candidates and criminals,
address eternity. But we
have already lived a long dream,
longer than I dreamed it could be.
I cannot predict the future
except that I know poetry

and love bestow such gifts that we
can never fully understand,
and so gather in gratitude:
Nine bows! Salutations! Praise!

→>-<←

Shiawase (1)

Epithalamion for Seki Yuko, October, 1995

Rising before five
A.M., my bride and I crept
from your father's house

at first light of day
to go off to the temple,
cold coffee in hand,

to enjoy morning
sutra recitation. Gray
is not Buddhist, not

formally any-
way. But each was a moment
that will last always,

in the heart of my
rough old heart and in Gray's too,
because your father

has given us his
undying love and because
your grandfather carved

ten thousand Buddhas
while your grandmother shaped her
bonsai, her garden

the great metaphor
expressing her devotion,
and because you are

your mother's child you
have learned all this and much more.
And now you marry.

I would like to think
of you and your new husband
walking hand in hand

through cemetery
and damp, empty temple grounds
just before sunrise,

the sutras ringing
in your ears. I would like to
think that you might find

greatest happiness
in such eternal moments.
I would like to dream

of you attaining
such eternal joy in each
new day's endeavors.

Because you are you,
and because your father is
brother to my soul,

I think of you now
and always with memories
of laughter. Let tears

also be welcome,
and celebrate our blesséd
temporality.

Your generous heart
was born in generations
past. Your laughter will

be a gift to all
whom you have loved or will love—
grandparents, parents,

husband, children, friends.
Already the leaves begin
to fall. Already

this cold autumn moon.
Your happiness touches us.
I wish you morning
sutras, and diapers, and songs
that charm the moon all night long.

→‑‑←

Shiawase (II)

Epithalamion for Seki Sanae, October, 1996

Like Hitomaro
watching the lovely women
of the ancient court,

I watch from shadows,
never forgetting to note
the ceremonies

and the rituals
of our passing. I cannot
be more than a friend,

a passing shadow,
your father's literary
brother, an orphan

in this world who came
to learn more of family
from your family

than I can explain.
Your grandfather's ten thousand
hand-carved Buddhas stand

in my heart's temple.
And your grandmother's ancient
bonsai are a seed

that will only grow
to reach fruition when you
are grandmotherly

yourself, enriched by
all the lives and deaths that come
to define a life.

Up before sunrise
as usual, now I walk
in a predawn glow

through wet, fallen leaves
and the lengthening shadows
of my brief lifetime,

made rich beyond dreams
by your mother's sweet laughter
that is morning gold

and evening moonlight,
made richer yet by your father's
generosity

of time, affection,
and what we hold in common.
And you make me rich

with your happiness—
and maybe a little sad
when I realize

this world is a dream,
and in our brief awakening
within the dream

we come face-to-face
with our own deaths which we must—
we *must*—learn to live.

Hitomaro watched.
He could *only* watch, and make
a humble poem,

however courtly.
You are a court, a temple,
Kannon's own vessel

pouring morning dew.
I return to you the love
and gratitude learned

from you, held in trust
across windswept seas and years,
returned with a bow
and the heart's truest sutra:
many moons and simple songs.

---><-

To Eron on Her Thirty-second Birthday

When the last shadow
of the forest vanishes
under the broad wings
of the last river falcon,
I will be alone again.

All the rain forests,
the endangered species and
flora and fauna
bearing testimony found
in hydrocarbons of stone . . .

going, going, gone.
Thus all our good intentions
are moving along—
their going is our going,
each bound to the other by

shared impermanence.
There's nothing that's not Nature.
And yet we are moved
almost to tears by the thought
of the last salmon or whale,

last wolf in the wild,
last California condor.
With a veil of tears
we shroud the dead we've tortured,
building cathedrals of lies.

Here at Kage-an,
we've golden and black bamboo,
white blossoming moss,
dark-leafed Japanese maple,
irises just being born—

emptiness in each,
as in this transient world.
Rexroth asked whether
meaning has being. I ask
how tall can the foxglove grow.

How long can the crow
strut his stuff, or the robin
continue to sing
the sun down under the earth?
I want to live a moment

in that song, to die
in that moment afterward,
when daylight has gone,
the world embalmed with silence
until the first marsh frog calls.

How much grief can one
life sustain?—ask the Rabbi
of Auschwitz who died
with his dignity intact,
or ask Chuang Tzu who laughs

loud at the question.
"I am not ashamed," Merwin
wrote in a poem,
"of the wren's murders nor the
badger's dinners on which all

worldly good depends."
Apologies to the slug
dissolving slowly
in the garden, and to the
mosquito thoughtlessly slapped;

and praise to the rice,
praise to the wine and to songs
that follow after;

and praise for our suffering,
which ennobles all our joys.

I have no wisdom
to offer on your birthday,
but here is a song
to celebrate emptiness,
to celebrate years to come.

When I come at last
to be a passing shadow,
I'll sound like a whale,
and plunge deep into the past.
We are devoid, Carruth says,

of essences, thus
neither young nor old, male nor
female, flesh nor stone.
Happy birthday, my dear one.
What outlasts us is our love.

→-◄-

For Kyra Gray O'Daly

(born October 10, 1997)

Yellow maple leaves
are already falling through
baby Kyra's tears

-›-›-‹-

Lives & Works

Bidding Farewell to My Stepson

for Andrew Roney

Your monastic days
at Kage-an are over;
you enter a world
of solitary travel
that is a measure of growth,

outer and inner.
You will take your mother's heart
with you wherever
you may wander. My heart too
is companion to your search

to find your own life.
What I say in poetry
cannot otherwise
be said or else I'd say it
more simply. The poem says

what cannot be said
in prose. Perhaps verse requires
of its maker a
struggle to open the heart,
a vulnerability,

a belief that words—
at least it has been for me—
mean exactly what
they say. Thus I can now say,
simply and clearly because

the poem itself
so clarifies, you have been
both brother and son
these years we've spent together.
While you have not shared my love

of good rice wine, for
poetry or Delta blues,
or passion for work—
you *are* post-adolescent—
you have been good company.

Through difficult days,
you have proven yourself man
enough now to face
the world that lies before you.
Forget "success" and "failure."

Forget cars, money,
the empty views of others.
The heartbreak you'll know
begins and ends within you.
If you are the question, you

must be the answer.
An old man talks to the wind
young men sail kites in.
All my advice is worthless.
You know that. I must give it

nonetheless because
both your mother's heart and mine
will be your constant
companions, and even more
when we are gone. My brother,

my almost-a-son,
the only life that matters
is this one. Because
you carry our hearts, you must
be careful. But be foolish,

too, when that time comes,
be as wise as you can be.
Beyond the desert,

mountains and seas all arrive.
As you will learn much too soon,

our time is a gift
which, because it is so brief,
is very fragile.
What you give away is yours
forever. The rest is waste,

mere greed and squalor.
All you will ever require
is already there,
within you. Use it wisely.
It will not last forever.

>-<

Corinthian Suns:
A Letter to Olga Broumas

Above me, the sun.
And the sea's sound floods my veins
when winds lift their wings
high over tall evergreens
along the Pacific Rim.

Midwinter, I long
for the Corinthian sun,
to hear the Greek tongue,
the Mediterranean
light transparent blue and white.

But the clouds that come
inevitably sweep down
from the frozen north,
blanketing the sun in shades
of ominous gray and blue,

the day darkened by
midafternoon. So I stoke
the woodstove, Olga,
and curl up on my futon
with Elytis, Seferis,

Sikelianos,
Yanni Ritsos, Cavafy,
their voices merging
into a new Greek chorus
drinking Corinthian suns.

Where would I be now
without those Greeks in English,
without your labors
and passions, and Keeley's too,
and the late Philip Sherrard's.

I journeyed to Greece
more to visit the moderns
than the ancient ones
I came to translate later.
How can I come to thank you

enough for bringing
the brilliance of that Greek sun
into my winter?
Can you ever understand
what I felt so long ago

walking down Syngrou
Avenue with Seferis
ringing in my ears?
Even now, after fifteen
years, it brings me a shiver.

Like ancient Taoist
sages, these poets bring me
stoical solace,
light in the heart of darkness,
a Way in which to follow.

And you who have been
equally everpresent
cannot know—because
you are Greek you cannot know—
how this orphan's heart was shaped

not by the Greek tongue,
but by something still deeper,
the soul's own whisper,
perhaps, or simply the light,
the eternally Greek light

shining from within.
Heavy winds and rains batter
the house. But I'm gone.
I'm strolling down Pandrosou,
drinking Corinthian suns.

–›–‹–

Lives of a Poet:
From Ryōkan

I. from the Chinese

1.
No bird above the wild hills.
Garden leaves fall one by one.

Desolate autumn winds:
a man alone in thin black robes.

2.
Dawn, the shrine under silver snow,
trees flower white on the grounds.

Out in the cold, one small boy
throwing snowballs—all the world his own.

3.
Too stupid to live among men,
I pass my years among herbs and trees;

too lazy to learn right from wrong,
laugh at me and I laugh along.

These old bones still cross the river,
begging-bag in hand, loving springtime weather.

I manage to survive.
I never once despised this world.

4.

Nothing satisfies some appetites,
but wild plants ease my hunger.

Free of untoward desires,
all things bring me pleasure.

Tattered robes warm frozen bones.
I wander with deer for companions.

I sing to myself like a crazy man,
and children all sing along.

5.

I never longed for the wilder side of life.
Rivers and mountains were my friends.

Clouds consumed my shadow where I roamed,
and birds pass high above my resting place.

Straw sandals in snowy villages,
a long walking stick in spring—

I sought a timeless truth: the flowers' glory
is just another form of dust.

6.

Young, I sat long hours of zazen
to master each quiet breath.

Snows and stars were my texts,
hunger and sleep unnoticed.

What peace my heart knows now
I owe to the discipline of youth. Yes, seek.

But lacking the artless art, each lesson
learned but once, who am I to preach?

7. *For the New Year*

Life bolts like a horse through a gate.
Year by year, we pile the debts we've wrangled.

Tomorrow begins another year
and I'm already grizzled and bedraggled.

The river willows wave their arms,
plums perfume the mountains.

I haven't wings to fly against the storm,
but like a phoenix, lift my voice to sing.

8.
I know a gentleman poet
who writes in the high old way—

master of form from Han and Wei
or new-style modeled on the T'ang.

With elegant strokes he quietly composes,
deftly adding images to startle.

But he hasn't learned to speak from the heart—
all wasted! Though he writes all night long.

9.
As a boy, I studied literature
but failed to become a scholar.

I sat for years in zazen,
but failed my Dharma Master.

Now I inhabit a hut
inside a Shinto shrine:

half common custodian,
half prophet of the Buddha.

10.
Sixty years a poor recluse alone
in a hut near a cliffside shrine.

Night rains fall and carve the cliff.
On the sill, my candle sputters in the wind.

11.
The winds have died, but flowers go on falling;
birds call, but silence penetrates each song.

The mystery! Unknowable, unlearnable.
The virtue of Kannon.

12.
Illusion and enlightenment are mutually entangled;
means and end, cause and effect are one.

Dawn to dusk, I study wordless texts in silence;
nights are lost to thoughtless meditation.

Warblers sing in the willows.
Dogs bark late in the moonlit village.

All emotions rise in a whirl.
I leave this old heart to the world.

13.
You stop to point at the moon in the sky,
but the finger's blind unless the moon is shining.

One moon, one careless finger pointing—
are these two things or one?

The question is a pointer guiding
a novice from ignorance thick as fog.

Look deeper. The mystery calls and calls:
no moon, no finger—nothing there at all.

14.
His cane he carved from rabbit-horn,
his robes he wove from air.

His sandals came from tortoise-wool.
He sang his poems with silent mouth

so everyone could hear.

II. from the Japanese

1.
Was it all a dream—
I mean those old bygone days—
were they what they seemed?
All night long I lie awake
listening to autumn rain.

2.
What might I leave you
as a last gift when my time
comes? Springtime flowers,
the cuckoo singing all summer,
the yellow leaves of autumn.

3.
All "three thousand worlds"
are summoned here together
by this falling snow,
this snow that lightly covers
all three thousand worlds and more.

4.
Ryōkan, if
anyone should ask, had
these last words for the world:
Namu Amida Butsu—
and offered nothing more.

➤─◄

Elegy:
Kawamura Yoichi (1932–1995)

They were utterly
beautiful, those ancient songs
from the *Man'yōshū*
sung by Kawamura-san
in a resonant deep voice

through a veil of tears
brought on by Hitomaro's
elegies, sorrows
resounding through a thousand
generations. The full moon

slowly rose and set
high over Kawamura-
san, the dark mountain
I named after my dear friend
who was teacher and brother.

And now I cannot
think of Hitomaro's dusk
beside the Ōmi
Sea without remembering
those nights in Hanamaki

and Yoichi's tears
and laughter and hot sake,
and long afternoons
sitting before the Go board.
The rose of Hanamaki

is suddenly gone.
And this world is more alone
than ever before,
his soft, impassioned voice lost
among the antiquities

and hosts of poets
he adored. Give me my cup
and my *tokkuri*—
my gift from Brother Yusuke—
and, *dōzo*, heat the sake.

My brother is dead.
And we are left to find ourselves
among ten thousand
things. Raise the cup and the voice
again and again and sing

back those bygone days:
he was Hitomaro's boy.
Sing me through my tears
with those ancient elegies.
Yoichi was such a joy.

+>-<+

The End of Winter:
Odysseas Elytis (1911–1996)

"Everything I love
is forever being born."
The end of winter.
The sage of Iráklion
liked to quote Hērakleitos,

"Extinguish hubris,
not fire," as he did that night
at the beginning
of winter twelve years ago.
His shadow in olive groves

will last forever,
the eternally Greek light
of his voice reveal
all that is Aegean—blues
and whites and unvarnished truths:

Little Mariner
or Maria Nephele,
the soul's companion,
Odysseas Elytis
is gone. The end of winter:

vernal equinox.
The little garden Buddha
wears a robe of moss.
Daffodils are pushing up,
and plum trees begin to bud.

A conscience arose,
body of light and wonder,
and heard the Sirens
as the sea winds carried him.
His song goes out and returns

in evening foghorns,
the cry of the gull or loon,
noble as Homer,
old as slowly breaking dawn.
The owl is gone. His fire burns on.

＋＞＜＋

Heart of Bamboo:
Two Letters to Christopher Yohmei Blasdel

I.

Play *Sanya* for me,
carry me back once again
on that timeless breath
through passionate ancient days
of wisdom, awe, and wonder.

Return me again,
deliver me to that world
beyond time and grief
where the deliberate breath
begins in the bamboo heart

and moves out slowly,
steadily, mysterious
as mountains in mist,
each note filled with *mono no
aware*, the beautiful

sadness of all things
in this so-temporal world.
The wisteria
blossoms again, and blossoms
fall. And we are somehow moved

to tears once again.
When snow and darkness cover
the western mountains,
I turn again to *Man'yō*
poets and their songs to find

the ancient order,
the path that winds through the heart
to lay it open
for all who follow behind.
The heart is sometimes a snare.

It wears disguises.
It tells us lies. It pretends
it does not know. It
invents what we want to hear
when we are snared by desire.

Strip away the words
for me again. Return me
to that world beyond
words, which are only
a reflection of desire.

A low moan gropes forth
from your *shakuhachi* and
the words fall away
like wisteria blossoms
and I am left to wander

the vast expanses
of the hearts of old masters.
You are a master,
my brother, you are a gate
and your breath is a temple.

Play a single note—
it is always that simple:
the heart can equate
more easily, more clearly,
with pure sound than with "meaning."

Play a single note
and reveal the truth therein.
The heart is a gate
only the breath passes through—
emptiness to emptiness.

The heart and the breath
are one. Play *Sanya* for me.
Play it one more time.

Winter comes to Kage-an,
cold rain in the great cedars.

Play *Sanya* for me
and I will recite again
the songs of Ikkyū,
Hitomaro or Ryōkan.
Autumn nights grow cold and long.

Each time I listen,
I hear you for the first time
all over again
and my heart goes out to greet
the thousand gifts you've given me.

II.
Yakamochi wrote
of the *hototogisu*,
the mountain cuckoo
who lays her egg in the nest
of the warbler, *uguisu*,

and departs, leaving
the little mountain warbler
to act as broodhen,
hatching and feeding the young
bird, treating it as her own.

Issa would be charmed
to think of stepmother bird
and stepchild singing,
each by each, its own strange song.
And we are strange birds also,

wind and rain rattling
or whispering from the heart
of ancient bamboo,
each of us nursed by a muse
leading us into mountains

we might never have
imagined—you with your song
and breath of bamboo,
me with my ghosts and prophets
of the utter emptiness.

When Sō Shi's great bird
looks down, all he sees is blue—
blue sky above, blue
sky below. In the perfect
world, it is "the bluest blue

of the heavens." Yet
the cicada and the dove
both laugh, "When we fly,
we don't kick up heavy dust!
It's easy to reach low trees."

Perhaps it's the old
feminine spirit who lives
on Ku She Mountain,
she who sips the morning dew,
who binds us close together.

You are my brother,
in whose nest I've placed an egg,
whose song is my song
because it is everyone's.
Or perhaps it is Kannon,

she who listens, she
who hears the cries of the world,
who has given us
this measure, this struggle for
song in a suffering world

not of our making.
We must carry the shadows
of the dead with us

wherever we may journey.
And we must carry the light.

It is only right
that we should be so burdened,
we who are foolish
with endless desire to know.
Yakamochi or Bashō,

Sō Shi or Issa,
I bow to the old masters.
And I bow to you
who have brought me much closer
to that art that is not art,

the heart of bamboo,
the silence that is the warp
for the weft of song.
We are strange birds in strange nests,
but the song is all our own.

→>-<←

The Lotus Sutra Revisited:
Two Letters to Keida Yusuke

1.
The great dharma wheel
turns inevitably on—
cherry blossoms fall,
covering Honjōji's pond,
dancing in the air like snow.

It has been just so
for a thousand years or more.
Now I come alone
in the predawn glow to bow
in memory of one who's gone

down that ancient road
each of us travels alone.
Young monks are chanting
the *Hokkekyō* in voices
beyond the measure of time.

Whatever I know
or think or feel is no use
to Yoichi now.
Long-life sutra or short-life
sutra—all the same somehow.

Out behind the hall,
Kannon stands alone among
cemetery stones,
in her hand a lotus bud
and upon her lips that smile.

She knows it is we
who most need compassion now.
Kannon Bosatsu,

tucked behind these Shingon grounds,
give me sweet solace and more:

at dawn in Sanjo,
blossoms bloom and fall;
I bow as I pass,
a pilgrim alone, going
I-don't-know-where-at-all.

2.
All evening long
I drink sake with Yusuke—
"Ten Thousand Mirrors
of Happiness," cold and sweet,
made by his new family—

talking poetry
late into the night. We miss
our brother's laughter,
his deep, authentic delight
in simply being alive.

This is our sutra,
our homage: *Man'yō* poets
sang the same praises
for all those who passed before.
It has been so a thousand

years and more. We raise
a cup to toast *tsubaki*
flowers as they fall. The moon
that rises is the same moon

Hitomaro praised
shining over Yoshino,
the same pale half-moon
that shone on Bashō's journey
through the wilds of Tohoku.

It is good to grieve.
But now our grieving is done.
The Lotus Sutra
brings it all back home: this world
is a world of suffering

and transcendence. Be
still. Breathe deeply. Pilgrimage
has no beginning
and no end. Only this song,
only this gratitude endures.

→>-<+-

Lives of a Poet:
Four Letters to Hayden Carruth

1.
A friend has sent me
a copy of your *Dark World*,
a mysterious
slender little Kayak book
from the indefatigable

George Hitchcock down in
Santa Cruz and printed by
Panjandrum Press in
that pale, inimitable,
almost ugly Hitchcock style.

That was twenty-two
years ago. You don't even
list *Dark World* on your
curriculum vita now.
Even then you were not young.

I guess you never
could be, so full of advice
culled from the classics,
so full of good sound common
and uncommon sense, furies

inspired by a love
that simply would not be dammed.
Bless you, dear Hayden.
I'm glad you followed your own
advice: "Reticence be damned."

2.
Pilate asks, "What is
love?" For which I substitute
friendship, which is love
unburdened by erotic
passion, but informed by love's

kindliness, if not
by the inevitable
necessities of
dialectic argument.
And so I begin again—

"My dear friend," I say,
meaning I have stood breathless
before the severe
beauty and anguish and love
and delight in your poems,

stood breathlessly still
as I listened to the turn
of a line or phrase
or flinched in recognition
of a painful truth revealed.

I do not know why
we must do it, why the line
begins somewhere in-
side the mind, its insistent
music delivering us

into another
world where the poem unfolds
from within, telling
us what's really on our minds.
I swear it is so. I've sworn

allegiance before—
not to some bloody old flag

snapping in the wind,
and certainly not to that
junkyard dog, the Patriot—

but to what can be
found in poetry: friendship
and small dignities,
evidence of a long life
lived with an ear to the wind

and a heart exposed.
I swear it's always been so.
A heart or poem
cannot be closed completely.
The heart of Hērakleitos

or Euripedes,
like the rhythms of Sappho,
resounds in your lines
as surely as the weather
of an age. And so I go

there in search of the
old familiar, the trusted
thing, the poem as
continuing thread binding
friend to friend across centuries.

Friendship is solace,
the root of a good marriage.
I extend my hand,
unwashed, still bloody with all
the excesses of our age.

I stand before your
poems as before a great
hearth in deep winter,
comforted by your labors.
I find sanctuary here.

We have our Pilates'
clean hands in public office.
We have messiahs
aplenty. I'm sick to death
of all those who want glory.

This is *poetry*.
It may change a life or burn
white-hot with passion;
it may bring a smile
or be a coat for Jacob
wandering the wilderness,

but you and I know
that lust for fame is folly.
You ought to have a
Nobel Prize, a Pulitzer,
all the honors in the world.

But that is not why
you write. For which act my heart
goes out to you who
helped me learn to open it.
For which act you are my friend

forever, doing
the real work of poetry.
Fuck money. Fuck fame.
There are three worlds. In this one,
gratitude flows like honey.

The suffering world
brings about its own demise.
This world is neither
fair nor wise, but paradise
reveals itself in every line.

What, finally, *is* love?
Willingness to face the end

without blinking? The
gift made—and given freely.
I bow to the poem, my friend.

3.
Wily Su Tung-p'o
observed of Wang Wei's landscapes,
"All of his paintings
contain poems; all of his
poems contain the essence

of paintings." Thus said,
he pointed toward balance
to find harmony.
In one inch of snow, tulip
bulbs at Kage-an frozen,

the woodpile a block
of ice to be chipped with my
splitting maul, little
raccoon tracks around the back
door and down the frozen steps

and off into woods
that creak with the shift of winds,
I attend my chores,
muttering against the cold
furies of northern winter.

You who love the snow
can have it. And you can have
the chainsaw poems
and marvelous descriptions
of Nor'east country townsfolk

in all their glory.
Just send me the warmth of rain.
"Sin is not so much

knowing (if it were, every-
body would be innocent)

as wanting to know."
Thus you quote Camus on sin.
I suppose my sin
has been relentless wanting
to know, whereas what I want

most to know right now
is comfort in married life,
the garden in spring,
the work at hand. This bloody,
bitter weather gets me down.

In my sins are all
my virtues, in my virtues
all my sins, for which
I can make no excuses:
I balance above the abyss.

This landscape is etched
in my blood—wouldn't have it
any other way.
This snow won't last, and neither,
happily, will you or I.

So I turn to your
cold weather poems, your thoughts
on sin and virtue
or on temporality.
Not for comfort exactly,

but because the truth
of the matter is, like that
other Williams—Hank—
I get so doggone lonesome—
and there you are, with woodsmoke,

almost three-quarters
of a century, and yet
the poems go on,
footsteps leading through the snow
until they become the snow.

You, like Su Tung-p'o,
are a master, a wily
old fox in the storm,
footsteps leading through the snow
until they become the snow.

4.
Reading your *Scrambled
Eggs & Whiskey*, I took note:
"The great poems of
our elders in many tongues
we struggled to comprehend

who now are content
with mystery simple and
profound..." and isn't
that the greatest mystery
of all? That we can at last

find within ourselves
a mundane ecstasy, or
simple contentments
known only in poverty
and at the price of patience—

which isn't my strong
suit, or so I always thought
until I awoke one day
and—sure enough—white whiskers
on a wizened, tired face.

Only then did I
begin to realize what I'd believed
all along: that joy
is not the orgasmic cry
in the night, nor lovely sighs

following after—
which are a mystery them-
selves, albeit thin
and fragile as a moth's wing
in flickering candlelight—

I wrote of Tu Fu
years ago, "His joys were neither
large nor many, but
they were precise." A moment
of prescience perhaps? Or
just the inevitable

result of struggling
to comprehend the tongue of
such a great master?
Probably both. In such great
and noble struggle I come

face-to-face with my
own small, quiet ecstasies
over a poem
that says for me what I could
not otherwise find true words

to say. Carruth or
Tu Fu, Sappho, Seferis—
it doesn't matter:
the poem somehow reveals
its particularities

and I am brought down
to my knees in gratitude
for the gift received.
If I am content at all,
it is because I struggled

all those many years,
because I was so foolish
then as to believe
that poetry was enough
to teach me to live, to love.

→-⤜

Notes

"The Fool": Bodhidharma is credited with bringing Buddhism to China in the 5th century C. E. His experience of sitting zazen for nine years is turned into a *kōan*, a "case" or question drawn from an episode in the life of a previous master, in the *Wu-men-kuan* (*The Gateless Barrier*). Ch'an Master Yang-ch'i (992–1049) was founder of the Yōgi school of Rinzai Zen. Although at one time an actual region in China, by the time of Chuang Tzu (3rd century B.C.E.), Yueh was referred to as an almost mythical time and place in antiquity. *Obaka* may be translated as big "dimwit" or "fool." Appearances aside, the name was given to me as an honorific echoing the nickname of the great poet Ryōkan, "Daigu," which means "big fool."

"After Po Chu-i": (772–846) One of the great poets of the T'ang dynasty and a major influence on succeeding generations of poets all across East Asia; some 2,800 of his more than 10,000 poems survive. Arthur Waley translated many of his poems.

"Three Worlds": Drawn from the Sanskrit "Three Worlds, Three Spheres," the Three Worlds of Buddhism are the World of Desire, the World of (transcendent) Desirelessness, and the World Beyond Form (or pure spiritual continuum). *Tsubaki* is a kind of camellia.

"After Yuan Chen": (779–831) He shared with his friend Po Chu-i a profound sense of social conscience and suffered exile for the crime of speaking out. I translated several of his famous elegies in *Midnight Flute*. An autobiographical piece by Yuan Chen became the basis for the classic *Dream of the Red Chamber*.

"A Warbler's Song in the Dusk": Otomo no Yakamochi (716–785) was one of the editors and principle contributors to the first Japanese Imperial poetry anthology, *Man'yōshū*, and these *waka* (short poems in syllabic lines of 5-7-5-7-7) are drawn from Chapters 17–20. These poems fall somewhere between translation, interpretation, and imitation. The *uguisu* (pronounced *oo-gweese*) is a Japanese warbler.

"Two Pines": Yung Chia (d. 713) was an early Ch'an master. I translate his Chinese quatrain into a Japanese *waka* (or modern *tanka*) because it parallels the second poem, written by his contemporary, Hakutsu (ca. 700), a Japanese Buddhist monk.

"After Han Yu": (768–824) Orphaned at three, Han Yu was self-educated and became a major poet, essayist, and literary theorist. A devout Confucian, he subordinated traditional literary formalities to exactitude of image and idea. (See especially "Poem on Losing One's Teeth" in Kenneth O. Hanson's *Growing Old Alive: Poems of Han Yu*.)

"By the Rapids": Drawn from the Chinese style poems (*kanshi*) of Sugawara Michizane (845–903), the first major Japanese poet to write Chinese-style poems. His best were modeled on the poetry of Po Chu-i. Michizane is a kind of saint of scholarship in Japanese culture. But even here, Chuang Tzu stands at the headwaters.

"Two Songs for Takamura Kotarō": One of the major Japanese poets and artists of the first half of this century, Kotarō studied sculpture with Rodin in Europe, and was among the first to bring vernacular Japanese into poetry. He married an artist, Naganuma Chieko, who went mad. His best poetry chronicles her gradual breakdown, and, later, his deep remorse over having supported Japanese nationalism. His little house in Japan's Tohoku country not far from Kitakami is now a museum. Chieko's famous paper cutouts predate those of Matisse. Kotarō's poems have been translated by Soichi Furuta and by Hiroaki Sato.

"Talking to Myself": Chao-chou (778–897) was one of the most important early Ch'an masters. Many of his kōans are collected in the *Wu-men-kuan*. "The road to T'ai-shan" refers to the way to "Heaven's Mountain," figurative center of Buddhist enlightenment in ancient China. "The Madman of Chu," Chieh Yu, makes several appearances in *Chuang Tzu*.

"Passing Through": "Today, today too, / somehow getting by these days, still / living in a haze." (See *The Spring of My Life*, and the notes for "Heart of Bamboo," in this collection.)

"The Oracle at Sunrise": The Didots, Bodoni, et alia, are masters of typography, printing, and traditional Western book design.

"Moon-Watching Pavilion": The "perfection of wisdom," is from the *Prajnaparamita Sutra,* a collection of about forty sutras, including *The Heart Sutra* and *The Diamond Sutra,* primary texts for Mahayana Buddhism.

"To Kenneth Rexroth": Adi-Buddha is Samantabhadra, a primary bodhisattva in Mahayana Buddhism, "He Whose Beneficence Is Everywhere." He is often depicted with a blue body in erotic union with a white consort. The "Gopis" are the ten thousand milkmaids with whom Krishna is said to have made love in a single night of ecstasy.

"To Gary Snyder": Zen master Dōgen (1200–1253) founded the Sōto school of Zen in Japan. He was a prolific writer and a profoundly original thinker revered as a bodhisattva by all the Buddhist branches. He is said to have read Chinese poetry fluently at age four. He edited and wrote commentaries on 300 kōans, and his *Shōbōgenzō* is one of the most influential documents on Zen. He advocated *shikantaza,* "nothing but precisely sitting" zazen—free of counting breaths or kōan pointers—just sitting *sitting.*

"Hitomaro's Song": Kakinomoto no Hitomaro (ca. 700) was the first major poet of the *Man'yōshū,* and the first "deified" poet of Japan.

"Ikkyū's Song of the Dream Garden": Ikkyū Sōjun (1394–1481) was one of Japan's greatest Zen masters, a great poet, musician, and calligrapher. He scandalized the Buddhist community when, at seventy, he fell in love with a blind singer forty years his junior and moved her into his quarters in the temple.

"Midaregami": The title ("Disheveled Hair") comes from the best-known volume of tanka by Japan's first major modern feminist, Yosano Akiko (1878–1942). She was one of the most remarkable women in the history of literature. See my *River of Stars: Selected Poems of Yosano Akiko* (translated with Keiko Matsui Gibson). My poem is loosely based upon classical Chinese structure rather than on the *form* of her tanka.

"Shiawase (i & ii)": In Japanese it means simply, "good fortune." But in early usage it often suggested good fortune that is a result of good karma. These poems were written on request for the weddings, one year apart, of the two daughters of my Japanese brother—teacher and translator, poet, high school principal, editor and Kerouac scholar—Keida Yusuke. Kannon (Japanese) is Kuan Shih Yin (Chinese) ("She Who Perceives the World's Cries"), usually depicted as a female bodhisattva of compassion, sometimes pouring the morning dew from a vessel, a small child clinging to her robe.

"Bidding Farewell to My Stepson": Kage-an is the name my wife and I have given to our studio, "Shadow Hermitage."

"Corinthian Suns": Odysseas Elytis and George Seferis are Greek Nobel Prize winning poets; Cavafy, Sikelianos, and Ritsos are also major modern Greek poets. Elytis told me during a visit to Athens in 1983, "A *real* poet needs an audience of three; since any poet worth his salt has two intelligent friends, one spends a lifetime looking for the third reader." Syngrou Avenue in Athens figures in the poetry of Seferis (see the *Collected Poems* translated by Edmond Keeley and Philip Sherrard); Pandrosou Street, a narrow shopping district for tourists in Athens, figures in the poetry of Elytis (see Keeley & Sherrard's translation of *Axion Esti* and Olga Broumas's translations, *Eros, Eros, Eros: Selected and Last Poems*).

"From Ryōkan" (1758–1831): A Zen monk in the Sōto school, Ryōkan lived by his begging bowl in a one-room hut on Mount Kugami in Japan's northeastern "snow country." He went to school on the *Man'yōshū*, and the poems of Han Shan (Cold Mountain), Su Tung-p'o, and the 12th-century Buddhist priest-poet Saigyō. Like Ikkyū before him, at an elderly age he fell in love with a young woman, in this case a Buddhist nun, with whom he exchanged remarkable poems. (See Burton Watson's *Ryōkan: Zen Monk-Poet of Japan*, and my *Only Companion*.)

"Elegy: *Kawamura Yoichi (1932–1995)*": He was my Japanese brother, teacher, and friend. He built a small addition on his little house in the mountains of Hanamaki-minami so I would have a place of my own to work while in Japan. In a chapter of *Bashō's Ghost*, I tell of his instrumental work in developing the Japanese National Modern Poetry Museum in Kitakami. He was a fine poet and editor, and his ear for incanting *Man'yō* poems was infallible. A *tokkuri* is the little jug for presenting sake, hot or cold.

"Heart of Bamboo": Christopher Yohmei Blasdel is a *shakuhachi* (Japanese bamboo flute) master who performs the classics as well as more modern improvisational and jazz work. Born in Texas, he has spent the last twenty-five years in Tokyo, where I first performed with him. Sō Shi is Chuang Tzu's name in Japanese (see *The Essential Chuang Tzu*, chapter one, for my quotes). Kobayashi Issa (1762–1826) was a haiku and haibun (prose and poetry combined) master equalled only by Bashō. His *magnum opus* is *Oraga haru* (see my translation, *The Spring of My Life*).

"*The Lotus Sutra* Revisited": *The Lotus Sutra* (*Hokkekyō* in Japanese) is the fundamental teaching of Buddhism, introducing the Four Noble Truths and the Eightfold Path (see Burton Watson's translation). Honjō-ji is a Shingon temple in Sanjo City, a short walk from the poet's home.

→>-<←

Acknowledgments

Grateful acknowledgment is made to the editors of the following journals in which several of these poems first appeared:

The American Poetry Review: "Preface: Ars Poetica," "Lives of a Poet: *Four Letters to Hayden Carruth*";
Blue Jacket (Japan): "Ten Thousand Mirrors of Happiness," "Shiawase (I & II)," "Elegy: Kawamura Yoichi";
Chicago Review: "After Coltrane's 'I'll Get By'";
Five Points: "The End of Winter," "Shunga," "A Thousand and One Tales";
Japan Environment Monitor: "After Po Chu-i," "Three Worlds";
Many Mountains Moving: "Lives of a Poet: *A Letter to Gary Snyder*";
Ploughshares: "The Fool";
Sei-en (Japan): "Salutation, Late Autumn, 1991";
Spillway: "The Art of Literary Exegesis," "The Art of Literary Translation," "Anti-Muse," "After Yuan Chen";
Shambhala Sun: "Talking to Myself";
Whelks Walk Review: "Lives of a Poet: *Ikkyū's Dream Garden*";
Rattle: "To Eron on Her Thirty-second Birthday".

Several of these poems originally appeared in the following books: *A Dragon in the Clouds* (Broken Moon Press, 1989) *animae* (Copper Canyon Press, 1980); *Mandala* (Milkweed Editions, 1991); *Living Light* (Jawbone Press, 1977); *Fatal Pleasure* (Breitenbush Publications, 1984); *The Nootka Rose* (Breitenbush Publications, 1987); *The Erotic Spirit* (Shambhala Publications, 1995); *Only Companion* (Shambhala Publications, 1992, 1997). Many have been revised for this volume.

+>-<+

About the Author

Sam Hamill is the author of more than thirty volumes of poetry, translations from ancient Chinese, Japanese, Greek, and Latin, and three collections of essays. His recent books include *The Gift of Tongues: Twenty-five Years of Poetry from Copper Canyon Press*; *The Erotic Spirit* (thirty centuries of erotic poetry); *Only Companion: Japanese Poems of Love and Longing*; *River of Stars: Selected Poems of Yosano Akiko* (with Keiko Matsui Gibson); *The Spring of My Life* (selected poems of Kobayashi Issa); *The Essential Chuang Tzu* (with J. P. Seaton); *The Essential Bashō*; and *A Poet's Work: The Other Side of Poetry* (Second Edition). His *Destination Zero: Poems 1970–1995* received a Pushcart Prize, among several honors. Hamill has been the recipient of fellowships from the National Endowment for the Arts, the Guggenheim Foundation, the U.S.-Japan Friendship Commission, the Andrew Mellon Fund, and the Lila Wallace-Readers Digest Foundation. He is Contributing Editor for *The American Poetry Review*, directs the Port Townsend Writers' Conference, and is Editor at Copper Canyon Press. He lives near Port Townsend, Washington.

→►◄←

BOA EDITIONS, LTD.: AMERICAN POETS CONTINUUM SERIES

Vol. 1   *The Fuhrer Bunker: A Cycle*
          of Poems in Progress
          W. D. Snodgrass

Vol. 2   *She*
          M. L. Rosenthal

Vol. 3   *Living With Distance*
          Ralph J. Mills, Jr.

Vol. 4   *Not Just Any Death*
          Michael Waters

Vol. 5   *That Was Then: New and*
          Selected Poems
          Isabella Gardner

Vol. 6   *Things That Happen Where*
          There Aren't Any People
          William Stafford

Vol. 7   *The Bridge of Change:*
          Poems 1974–1980
          John Logan

Vol. 8   *Signatures*
          Joseph Stroud

Vol. 9   *People Live Here: Selected*
          Poems 1949–1983
          Louis Simpson

Vol. 10 *Yin*
          Carolyn Kizer

Vol. 11 *Duhamel: Ideas of Order in*
          Little Canada
          Bill Tremblay

Vol. 12 *Seeing It Was So*
          Anthony Piccione

Vol. 13 *Hyam Plutzik: The Collected*
          Poems

Vol. 14 *Good Woman: Poems and a*
          Memoir 1969–1980
          Lucille Clifton

Vol. 15 *Next: New Poems*
          Lucille Clifton

Vol. 16 *Roxa: Voices of the Culver*
          Family
          William B. Patrick

Vol. 17 *John Logan: The Collected Poems*

Vol. 18 *Isabella Gardner: The*
          Collected Poems

Vol. 19 *The Sunken Lightship*
          Peter Makuck

Vol. 20 *The City in Which I Love You*
          Li-Young Lee

Vol. 21 *Quilting: Poems 1987–1990*
          Lucille Clifton

Vol. 22 *John Logan: The Collected Fiction*

Vol. 23 *Shenandoah and Other Verse Plays*
          Delmore Schwartz

Vol. 24 *Nobody Lives on Arthur*
          Godfrey Boulevard
          Gerald Costanzo

Vol. 25 *The Book of Names:*
          New and Selected Poems
          Barton Sutter

Vol. 26 *Each in His Season*
          W. D. Snodgrass

Vol. 27 *Wordworks: Poems Selected and New*
          Richard Kostelanetz

Vol. 28 *What We Carry*
          Dorianne Laux

Vol. 29 *Red Suitcase*
          Naomi Shihab Nye

Vol. 30 *Song*
          Brigit Pegeen Kelly

Vol. 31 *The Fuehrer Bunker:*
          The Complete Cycle
          W. D. Snodgrass

Vol. 32 *For the Kingdom*
          Anthony Piccione

Vol. 33 *The Quicken Tree*
          Bill Knott

Vol. 34 *These Upraised Hands*
          William B. Patrick

Vol. 35 *Crazy Horse in Stillness*
          William Heyen

Vol. 36 *Quick, Now, Always*
          Mark Irwin

→-◄-

Colophon

Gratitude, poems by Sam Hamill, has been typeset using
Monotype Dante fonts and Rococo Ornaments, and issued
in a first edition of 2,250 copies, of which 2,200 trade
copies are bound in paper.

Twenty-six copies, bound in quarter cloth and French papers
over boards, lettered A–Z, and signed by the poet,
are for sale to the trade.

An additional twenty-four copies, also bound in quarter cloth
and French papers over boards, numbered
I–XXIV, signed by the poet, and including a poem
in holograph, are reserved by the publisher for
presentation purposes.

⤝⤞⤟